LOCKHEED
F-117
NIGHTHAWK

An Illustrated History of the Stealth Fighter

Bill Holder & Mike Wallace

Schiffer Military/Aviation History
Atglen, PA

Dedication

To Ben Rich

Acknowledgements

Captain Tracy O'Grady-Walsh, ASC Office of Public Affairs
Diana Cornelisse, ASC History Office
David Menard, Air Force Museum Research Department
Spencer P. Lane, Amos Newspapers
Lockheed Public Relations Office
Gary Creiglow, Former F-117 SPO employee
Larry O'Grady, Former F-117 SPO employee
Captain Marcel Kerdavid, Desert Storm F-117 pilot
Captain Rob Donaldson, Desert Storm F-117 pilot
LeRoy Stout, Air Force Museum volunteer

Cover photo courtesy of Rick Llinares, Flightline Photography

Book Design by Ian Robertson.

Copyright © 1996 by Bill Holder & Mike Wallace.
Library of Congress Catalog Number: 96-07855

Printed in China.
ISBN: 0-7643-0067-9

We are interested in hearing from authors with book ideas on related topics.

Published by Schiffer Publishing Ltd.
77 Lower Valley Road
Atglen, PA 19310
Phone: (610) 593-1777
FAX: (610) 593-2002
Please write for a free catalog.
This book may be purchased from the publisher.
Please include $2.95 postage.
Try your bookstore first.

Chapter One
What is This Stealth?

"Stealthiness," or low observables technology, is a term with which the F-117 Nighthawk is most closely associated. In a general sense, stealth is a desired characteristic of any combat aircraft; the ability to attack a target and leave undetected means a high probability of mission success and survivability.

The concept isn't new. As we shall see, there were attempts at disguising aircraft by means of camouflage during World War I. Advances in technology—most notably radar—have given designers new technical problems to solve, but the primary aim of defeating enemy detection has stayed intact.

It should be noted that claims for stealth—especially modern low observables—are difficult to measure. There seems to be little argument that the United States has the lead in this set of technical disciplines, but the degree of effectiveness remains a mystery to the general public. However, stealth has been a design goal since early in the history of aerial combat, and the unqualified success of the F-117 in combat against ground targets in Baghdad lends credibility to stealth's worthiness.

Before stealth, there was camouflage. Many techniques were tried through the years. Here is one scheme tried on the B-1A bomber, circa 1981. (USAF Photo)

A (very) Brief History of Aerial Stealth

World War I, the "war to end all wars," saw the application of camouflage techniques mainly upon ground equipment—tanks, trucks, etc. Painting aircraft in ground camouflage schemes to protect aircraft caught parked on fields and at the mercy of the enemy, however, was done only to a limited degree.

In fact, anti-camouflage—bright colors and/or characteristic paint schemes, such as that of the crimson Fokker triplane of Baron Richtofen, were more the order of the day. Perhaps the rationale was that the characteristic red would announce the Baron and strike fear in his opponents. Another reason was that pilots assumed that, in general, when they were able to see an enemy plane, the enemy was likewise able to see them.

Tactics were more important than aerial camouflage. A pilot counted first on the element of surprise: if he spotted an enemy aircraft, he would climb up to prepare a dive out of the sun. The sun became the factor which disguised the attacking aircraft.

Reportedly, however, there was an attempt on the part of the Germans to disguise an aircraft by making it nearly transparent. The frame of a Fokker fighter was covered with a clear cellophane material. Of course, the frame members, engine, etc. were still visible. Airborne, the material was not up to withstanding the loads and its smooth surface reflected sunlight. The experiment was unsuccessful.

World War II brought about a variety of paint schemes—ground colors of browns and greens abounded, for example. Designers also applied light blue to underwing and lower fuselage areas and dark blues to above wing and upper fuselage in an attempt to protect especially carrier-based aircraft from visual detection. Eventually most U.S. aircraft went either that way or silver-gray.

An example of modern USAF camouflage is illustrated by this YF-22 prototype fighter which is a blended combination of grays. (Lockheed Photo)

The shortcoming of paint was that at a distance, against the sky, an aircraft looked more or less like a black dot regardless of how it was painted. For a cruising aircraft to defeat visual detection, the only surefire answer was to fly at night.

The technology of radar, however, took away the cover of darkness from night-flying aircraft, and it began to be used from both ground and aerial platforms.

"Radar" is an acronym for "radio detecting and ranging." In its basic form, it is an electronic device from which radio waves are transmitted. These radio waves travel in a straight line until they strike something and are reflected back to the device. The time it takes for the echo to return to the antenna gives an extremely accurate measure of distance of the ob-

A similar scheme made on to operation aircraft, such as this F-111E. (USAF Photo)

Flat black is another technique of camouflage as illustrated by this AV-8 Harrier. (US Marine Photo)

One of the greatest challenges of current fighter aircraft is the masking of infrared emissions. The AIM-7 Sidewinder, shown here on an F-16C, is one of the most successful IR-guided missiles in anyone's inventory. (USAF Photo)

ject from the device. The distance combined with the direction the antenna faces tells the radar operator nearly exactly where the target object is. The target looks like a dot on a screen.

During WWII, researchers devised a measure of stealth called radar cross section, or RCS. RCS became the strength of the radar echo from the target with that of a reflective sphere having a one-square-meter cross section.

Size was an important factor for radar detectability. Simply put, everything else being equal, the smaller an object, the more difficult it is to detect. Effective fighters and bombers could be only so small, however (Designing aircraft with smaller and smaller RCS led to the development of small-fuselage aircraft such as the very successful U-2 surveillance plane. Small RCS also was a factor in the development of remotely piloted vehicles—known later as unmanned aerial vehicles—which, despite meeting numerous design and operational performance goals, were discontinued).

Shape was important also. In their measurements of RCS, researchers found that a flying wing design resulted in an RCS smaller than what would be returned from a conventional shape. This idea, of course, led to Northrop's famous flying wing bomber designs of the early post-WWII era and

The AIM-9 Sparrow, shown here being launched from an F-18 Hornet, is a radar-guided air-to-air missile. Stealthy aircraft like the F-117A, unlike most other aircraft, are not fair game for this type of missile because of its low radar reflection. (US Navy Photo)

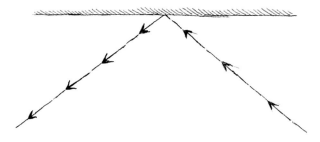

One of the ways to fool radar is to bounce the beams away from the radar source. (Wallace Drawing)

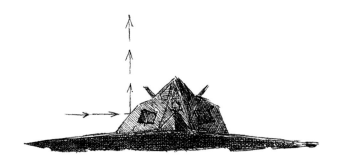

No surface on the F-117 is within 30 degrees of vertical. For that reason, radar beams are deflected off into space. (Wallace Drawing)

later to the Air Force B-2 bomber and Navy prototype A-12 fighter.

Another important factor was material—what the aircraft was made of or painted with made a difference in the RCS. Materials such as radar absorbent material (RAM) paint, a rubber matrix supporting aluminum flakes developed by the Massachusetts Institute of Technology near the end of WWII, showed promise. RAM reduces radar reflection and is inher-

ently a stealth technology (While this M. I. T. material was effective in some applications, it wasn't rugged enough for aircraft use. In fact most RAMs to this day aren't suited for aircraft use because they add too much weight or won't adhere properly. Research continues).

Reflecting radar waves is one problem for the would-be stealthy aircraft; another is infrared (IR) detection. This tech-

It's a planform that is totally different to those acquainted with current fighter designs. The stealth capabilities of the F-117 Nighthawk made it the star of Desert Storm. (USAF Photo)

Shown here, the F-117's multiple, slanted surfaces are highly visible. Because of this orientation and shaping, radar tracking is nearly impossible. (Lockheed Photo)

Conceived in the black, its flat black silhouette makes the F-117 hard to detect visually, and its faceted fuselage makes it even harder to detect with radar. (USAF Photo)

Developed later than the F-117, the YF-22 and YF-23 both exhibited some stealth chacteristics — but certainly nothing that even remotely resembles that of the F-117 (USAF Photo)

The Advanced Tactical Fighter Program, which was developed in the same time period as the F-117, was a much more open program. Artists' concepts submitted for the ATF program, such as this advanced concept from Grumman, were in stark contrast to the black secret world of the F-117. (Grumman Photo)

nology has resulted in equipment which "sees" differences in heat signatures, creates television-like pictures, and puts them on a screen. IR detection equipment makes it possible to track and target aircraft.

Defeating radar and IR systems were—and are—formidable tasks. Building aircraft having the ability to cruise undetected while in harm's way largely remained a goal rather than an accomplishment through the mid-to-late 1980s.

To be sure, U.S. aircraft did operate in environments which were dangerous due to ground-based detection and anti-aircraft artillery systems as well as enemy fighters. Flying tactics honed by rigorous pilot training and practice and electronic countermeasures bolstered by technological leaps in computing capabilities were important factors enabling these operations.

While the F-117 was designed with stealth as the primary characteristic, the YF-22 has many virtues in addition to stealth, including supersonic cruise and high maneuverability. Also the F-22 is primarily an air-to-air fighter, while the F-117 is air-to-ground. (USAF Photo)

At first glance, the B-2 stealth bomber, with its blended wing/ body and radar-absorbant coating, doesn't appear to re- semble the F-117. However, the zig-zag pattern of the engine inlet and other features that break up radar returns bear some similarity. (USAF Photo)

Another dramatic view of the B-2, taken under the nose and looking up, again shows some F-117 heritage with the zig-zag features. (USAF Photo)

TACIT BLUE, a stealth technology demonstrator, aided in stealth aircraft development. This once highly classified program ran from 1978 to 1985 as a joint Air Force/DARPA effort with Northrop as the prime contractor. It featured a straight tapered wing with a V tail mounted on an oversized fuselage with a curved shape. It had a wingspan of about 48 feet, a length of 55 feet, and weighed 30,000 pounds. A single flush inlet on the top of the fuselage provided air to two high-bypass turbofan engines. Only one complete airframe was ever flown, although a second airframe shell was constructed to serve as a backup. The vehicle is presently on display at the U.S. Air Force Museum at Wright-Patterson AFB, Ohio. (USAF Photo)

In Vietnam, for example, U.S. pilots learned to fly low towards their targets. In theory, the direction of enemy ground-based radar systems allowed flying space between the earth and the lowest point of the radar beams.

Flying low led to the development of terrain-following (TF) radar which made mission success and pilot survival a little more assured. Interestingly, it also led to radar detection systems which oftentimes caused pilots to turn off their TF systems.

Ground-based enemy radars became targets for systems such as the U.S. Air Force F-4G Wild Weasel aircraft. These fighters carried equipment which enabled them to "home in" on operating radars by following their beams to the source. Of course, in doing so, the F-4Gs were themselves targets (In the 1980s, the Air Force developed the TACIT RAINBOW, a missile which in tests successfully demonstrated its design capabilities of "loitering" after launch in an area suspected of having an "enemy" radar; when the radar began operating, the missile would fly itself at the radar. The system was never fielded, however.)

Although made famous in Desert Storm, F-117s perform just as well in a frigid atmosphere. (USAF Photo)

It follows that if one F-117 is hard to see, two F-117s will be equally tough to detect. (USAF Photo)

They look like the eyes of some alien being, but actually this is the head-on view of the Nighthawk. Note that there is hardly any reflection. (USAF Photo)

Actively suppressing ground radar by means of electronic jamming was the next step. The Air Force EF-111A Raven has this capability. Although very effective against ground-based systems, the application is somewhat limited and power demands are very high.

Defense against airborne (aircraft and later air-to-air missiles) radar relied upon detection of radar waves and dispersion of chaff. Chaff is thousands of tiny ribbons of foil. When scattered, they present so many false returns to the radar that targeting is impossible.

Infrared-guided, or "heat-seeking," missiles began to appear. After launch, these types of missiles "see" an IR image and fly themselves at the brightest spot—usually the exhaust outlet.

Countering the IR missile threat relied first upon detecting, by radar or visual means, the missile firing, and then flying towards the sun hoping that the sun's brightness would divert the missile into attacking it. Obviously, this was a day-time-only expediency.

A more recently developed counter is flares. The flares would act as miniature suns to confuse IR-guided missiles and could be used day or night.

While these defensive tactics are expedient, the fact that missiles are fired at all presupposes that the aircraft was detected already and that the enemy knows his airspace is penetrated.

In contrast, stealth technology is passive: no beams, no suppression, nothing to alert an enemy that something's afoot.

Stealth, as exemplified by the F-117 Nighthawk, is a blending of design and material technologies which makes it possible for the aircraft to fly anywhere virtually undetected by radar and infrared systems. In combat, it operates at night, making visual detection impossible. In Desert Storm, for example, F-117s carried out missions and escaped without so much as a single bullet hole in damage. Those accomplishments clearly demonstrated the value of stealth.

Chapter Two
Research, Design, and Development

Everything about the F-117 program seemed to have a sinister BLACK look and feel about it.

Of course, the plane was initially conceived, designed and developed as a BLACK Program, a super-secret program that by-passed the red tape that normally plagues Air Force weapon systems.

BLACK data point number two was the fact that this plane, in its operational configuration, is for the most part that opaque color.

Then, there is the environment in which this plane operates and where much of the test program was conduced — the BLACK of night. Because of those late hours, it was necessary for the test pilots to used BLACKed-out windows for sleeping.

Finally, any adversary that has to face this plane would certainly categorize it in the "BLACK Hat" category because of its nearly-unstoppable offensive capabilities. 'Nuff said!

There were a number of interesting aspects of the program — including the fact that the aircraft received an "F" designation even though it must be considered more of a bomber than a fighter. After all, the plane carries no offensive weapon systems (no guns, no missiles), just a pair of 2000-pound bombs as its main mission. About the only fighter characteristic is its diminutive size.

The Famous Photo Release

Of course, the release of that famous first F-117 picture in l988, which presented about as many questions as it answered, ended years of speculation on what this program was really all about.

To every observer, though, the amazing faceted shaping was quite a surprise. None of the "experts" that had predicted the F-117 shape even came close. Guesses about the flying wing shape of the B-2, which was released later, would be a lot closer.

Many issued a resounding sigh of relief when the release was made. Others, however, thinking that the release came as a result of political motivations rather than as a move in the national interest, thought it was a huge mistake that could possibly threaten national security. No matter what, it was definitely a tough decision to make.

News Release
United States Air Force

AERONAUTICAL SYSTEMS DIVISION, OFFICE OF PUBLIC AFFAIRS (ASD/PA)
WRIGHT-PATTERSON AFB, OH 45433 (513) 255-9493
PAM # 88-186

AIR FORCE DISCLOSES
STEALTH FIGHTER

WRIGHT-PATTERSON AFB, Ohio, Nov 10, 1988--The Air Force announced today the existence of an operational stealth fighter aircraft, officially known as the F-117A. The single seat, dual engine aircraft is built by the Lockheed Corporation in California. The F-117A first flew in June 1981.

The F-117A has been operational since October 1983, and is assigned to the 4450th Tactical Group at Nellis AFB, Nevada. The aircraft is based at the Tonopah Test Range Airfield in Nevada. A total of 59 aircraft are being procured. Fifty-two have already been delivered to the Air Force and seven more are in production.

With disclosure of the F-117A program, this mature system, which has enjoyed bipartisan congressional support since its inception, can now be fully integrated into operational plans in support of world-wide defense commitments. This system adds to the deterrent strength of U.S. military forces.

The F-117A program is managed at Aeronautical Systems Division, a major product division of Air Force Systems Command, headquartered at Andrews AFB, MD. Lt. Col. Ber Reiter is the program manager.
-30-

Contact: Capt. Tess Taft (513) 255-9493

Here it is! The first released photo of the F-117 was indeed a surprise — first that it was released at all, and second for the unexpected shape of the machine. (USAF Photo)

The official announcement accompanying the photo provided brief details on the program. (USAF Press Release)

U.S. Air Force Lockheed F-117A

The Lockheed prime contractor released this artist's concept in 1989. It depicted more clearly the details which were not clear in the first official photograph. (Lockheed Drawing)

Inside Lockheed's famous Skunk Works, the F-117 grew from this early wooden mockup. Even in this early design, the strange shaping that would characterize the Nighthawk were evident. (Lockheed Photo)

Gary Creiglow, who formerly headed the F-117 Air Crew Training Program, recalls the first time he saw the plane at an air show. "It was a strange feeling seeing the plane after all the secrecy for all those years," he revealed. "It was definitely the end of an era for a lot of folks who had worked on the program."

Even though there was great excitement after the photo release, there were political rumblings. In fact, right up until the time that the release was made, there were doubts about whether the release would actually take place. There were charges that the timing of the release was politically motivated; it was originally scheduled to take place just before the 1988 Presidential election. It actually took place two days after the election.

Actually, probably the largest motivation for the release was the need for night flying in the F-117 flight test program which presented additional dangers to the pilots. Had daylight flying been allowed, the unique shape would have been known much earlier.

Implications of the Photo Release
Though the print media had speculated through the years what the black machine would look like, the most vivid guesses came from a number of plastic model kits. The models' guesses were not even close to the actual shaping. Still, those old F-19 (guessed-at designation for the F-117) kits have become real collectibles, despite their bad guesses.

Perhaps as big a surprise as the shape itself was the designation the plane received. Many had speculated that it

would receive the next "F" number in line, i.e. the F-19 designation. But that would not be the case; it received the somewhat confusing F-117 nomenclature.

The F-19 designation actually never existed, since it was skipped to get to the F-20 designation used by Northrop for its aborted lightweight fighter development. Northrop wanted the number F-20 for its new program to give the impression that the aircraft represented the start of a new aircraft series. Of course, when the F-20 nomenclature was announced, there was even more speculation at the time that the F-19 was indeed the F-117's designation.

That F-117 three-digit number came from an earlier numbering sequence that started with an F-110 designation given to the F-4 Phantom when the Air Force adopted the new numbering system. Next followed the obvious F-111 fighterbomber. But the jump from the F-111 to the F-117 numenclature is a mystery. One theory is that the interim numbering could have come from the Air Force giving designations to Soviet aircraft that were being tested at the time. It might go something like this — F-112 (MiG-17), F-113 (MiG-19), F-114 (MiG-21), F-115 (MiG-23) and F-116 (Su-7/20). Just a guess, though!

Early Program Management
Interestingly, the F-117 didn't start as an Air Force program. It was initiated in 1976 as a Defense Advanced Research Projects Agency (DARPA) program on the suggestion of Lockheed executive Ben Rich. The official prime contract was issued to Lockheed in January 1977 and received the code name HAVE BLUE.

Shown here, technicians assemble the basic shell of an F-117. Only 59 were produced, each nearly a hand-built operation. (Lockheed Photo)

The F-117 undergoes non-destructive testing at the Sacramento Air Logistics Center. Without touching the aircraft, the inspection can quickly detect and identify cracks and other structural problems. The non-destructive testing includes ultrasonic inspection, fixed and maneuverable X-ray, and neutron radiography. (USAF Photo)

The initial contract was about as simple as you could get. Only several pages in length, the contract had only five specific requirements:

-Capability of carrying a pair of 2500-pound weapons (i.e. bombs)
-400 nautical mile radius
-Mach .9 cruise capability
-Operate from a NATO standard runway
-Achieve a specified level of stealth

The go-ahead for the F-117 program occurred at almost the same time that President Jimmy Carter took office. But later that same year it became apparent that the DARPA organization was not suited for a program of this magnitude. The Air Force Systems/Command at Andrews Air Force Base, Maryland, would become the responsive organization, which transferred the aircraft design and development overnight to the Aeronautical Systems Division (ASD) at Wright Patterson Air Force Base.

On July 12, 1990, General Michael Dugan, USAF Chief of Staff, accepted the 59th and last F-117A from Ben Rich, President of Lockheed Advanced Development Company. The ceremonies took place at the Lockheed plant in Palmdale, California. (USAF Photo)

After its release, the prime contractor, Lockheed, used the F-117 in a number of national advertisements. (Lockheed Advertisement)

When the Nighhawk came out of the black world, it drew huge crowds of spectators wherever it went. Here, an F-117 is on display at the United States Air and Trade Show in Dayton, Ohio in July 1990. Note that security is still maintained; a number of armed Air Force guards have their M-16s at the ready. (John Farquhar Photo)

Air Force Management

The overall management of the system took place from a Systems Project Office (SPO) obscurely located in Building I4 at Wright Patterson. Some of the original cadre of that deeply-secret operation recall some of the interesting operating modes from those exciting times in the late 1970s and 1980s.

Larry O'Grady, an auditing expert at the time, said that the SPO (which carried the early designation of YSX) was small compared with other SPO's. "Other offices at the time had about 600 personnel, the F-117 SPO only had about a hundred. Decisions were made quickly and there was a strong relationship between the project office and the contractors. The red tape, which is characteristic of many large aircraft programs, was practically non-existant in this program. Employees were given huge responsibilities and expected to get the job done with very little supervision. They did it well. That was one big reason that the program was successful.

"A decision would be made at at the Wright Patterson level and never be questioned in Washington. And another amazing thing about the operation was the fact that this super-important program was run by a Colonel. Never did get a General's slot back in those days," O'Grady explained.

Even though there was another stealth program (the B-2 bomber) also being carried out in a nearby building, O'Grady explained that there was very little similarity between the two programs. "The B-2 was a much bigger program with a different application," he said.

O'Grady indicated that even with the comparatively large number of personnel that carried the F-117 clearance, both government and contractor, the secret never got out. For security reasons, much of the interface work that was done between Air Force and the many contractors was done face-to-face, causing some pretty hefty travel costs.

"The unique shaping of the aircraft was the most important security aspect of the program," O'Grady indicated. That is, it was until that famous first fuzzy photo was released to the public.

Creiglow explained that after the release, employees were allowed to tell their families that this was the plane that they had been working on so secretively. "It was a relief to finally be able to say something," he confided. "For many many people working on the program, though, it was just as big a surprise because most of them had never seen a picture of the plane, either."

Both former F-117 employees told of the high priority given to recruiting the best people for the program. Creiglow explained, "When a person, either military or civilian, was interviewed for the F-117 program, there was no identification of the program to which he or she were going to be assigned. You took your chances, but you knew that it was something important.

"But make no mistake, this was a high-pressure, long-working-hours assignment, and there were many divorces

This photo shows an F-117 being pulled into position for display at an air show. (John Farquhar Photo)

that resulted from people working on that program through the years."

Particular attention was paid to the clearances of all the personnel that entered the F-117 program. Acquiring these clearances took a long time, especially for those who came to the program with no security clearance, making it tough on the fast-moving program.

The Air Force and the prime contractor got the job done in super fashion. Just look at the results! For their accomplishment, the Air Force/Lockheed team was awarded the coveted 1989 Robert J. Collier Trophy "for their work on the F-117A aircraft."

The Collier trophy is awarded for the greatest achievement in aeronautics or astronautics in America, demonstrated by actual use during the previous year. A citation which accompanied the trophy called the F-117 effort an accomplishment "which changes the entire concept of military aircraft design and combat deployment of the future."

Lockheed Design and Development

The Lockheed F-117 involvement actually began in the early 1970s when the company's famous Skunk Works, the developer of such famous aircraft as the SR-7l and U-2, became involved in the HARVEY program, which addressed early stealth concepts. The work resulted in the establishment of the Echo I computer program, the initial effort to simulate the effects of reduced cross-section vehicles.

The aforementioned HAVE BLUE program followed, with the construction of a subsonic, single-seat prototype powered by a pair of General Electric J85 powerplants. The design had the same overall shape as the final F-117 configuration, but lacked the angularity the characterized the final model.

A comparatively small aircraft, the HAVE BLUE was just over 47 feet in length, 7.5 feet tall, with a wingspan of 22.5 feet (about 40% the size of the final F-117 design).

But this was not your average aircraft — not even close! It was unique from a control point of view, with no lift devices, speed brakes, or flaps. The steel, aluminum and titanium structure accomplished control with inboard elevons and fins at the wing root. This was strictly a research aircraft, with no weapons bay that would be a part of the operational version. The HAVE BLUE aircraft did, however, carry a pitot tube, but it was retracted during periods of stealth testing. The 12,500-pound testbed also carried an advanced fly-by-wire guidance system.

During testing the HAVE BLUE vehicle demonstrated a 72.5 degree leading edge sweep, which resulted in a very low payload capability. In the final F-117 configuration, that angle was reduced by about five degrees. The design of the HAVE BLUE canopy was also extensively changed in the F-117 layout.

In retrospect, the HAVE BLUE aircraft would have only a passing resemblance to the final configuration. Still, its shaping was kept in high security. The first flight took place early in 1978.

Quite frankly, there was some real doubt among Lockheed engineers that the HAVE BLUE would be able to fly at all. Many, in fact, had commented that it was probably the ugliest airplane they had ever seen. Fighter aircraft are supposed to be sleek silver bullets, looking like Mach 2 just sitting there! The HAVE BLUE sure didn't have that appearance.

In May 1978, the HAVE BLUE program suffered a setback: the first model experienced a hard landing which jammed the right landing gear in a semi-deployed position. For safety reasons, it was decided to have the pilot eject. This resulted in the loss of the aircraft and injuries to the pilot.

The testing of the second HAVE BLUE test craft took place until the early 1980 time period, with strenuous testing of the

Capt. John Savage (left) and Sgt. Douglas Beck do a preliminary check of an F-117 stationed at Tonopah. (USAF Photo)

This early Nighthawk undergoes a pre-flight checkout prior to a test mission. (USAF Photo)

An F-117A stands on the flight line as part of a static display at the 1991 Paris Air Show. A GBU-27 is on display in front of the aircraft. (US Navy Photo)

aircraft's radar-reflecting capability. Modifications continued to be made to increase the effectiveness of that concept. That plane, however, was also lost in a crash.

There was a second little-known stealth program with military applications, this time for the US Navy. Unfortunately, according to officials at the Lockheed "Skunk Works" design facility, there was no interest from that branch of service, with no finished model ever being built. The vehicle to receive the F-117 stealthy look was actually a submarine with the same angled outer surfaces, only in this application having the capability to bounce off sonar signals. With the success the F-117 has enjoyed, one can wonder whether the Navy is having second thoughts now.

HAVE BLUE testing and the actual testing of the F-117 aircraft was carried out in a secret desert location in the western United States, known as Groom Lake. As was the case with all other planes of the program, secrecy was again the by-word of this location.

Groom Lake was actually a part of the Tonopah Test Range (TTR), in the far northwestern corner of Nellis Air Force Base, Nevada. Over the years, the area had seen a number of different advanced programs, but nothing like this. The location was excellent for the F-117 program because the huge unpopulated area allowed for mostly unobserved flight.

In 1994, the Air Force quietly acknowledged that Groom Lake had been the location where the U-2, A-12, SR-71, and of course, the F-117 were developed. The Air Force stated, "We do have facilities within the complex near the dry lakebed of Groom Lake. The facilities are used for testing and training technologies, operations and systems critical to the effectiveness of US military forces."

But curious aviation buffs knew much earlier that something was going on at the site. On several national TV shows, there were stories about people looking at the facility with long range telescopes. It is hard to keep something as exciting as the F-117A secret. Nonetheless, with this program, the job was accomplished.

To protect the great secret from the many prying eyes both in the air and on the ground, individual hangars were constructed at TTR for each aircraft. Ground personnel using only a flashlight guided the returning planes back to their hangars. After engines were shut down, and the aircraft blocked, the doors of the hangars were closed, lights turned off, and the business of preparing the fighter for its next flight was started. In addition, the unique camouflage paint scheme of the aircraft was intended strictly to help keep the flights away from public view.

The Lockheed kingpin in the F-117 development was Ben Rich, who passed away in January 1996 during the writing of this book. He was a methodical, no-nonsense engineer who knew how to manage the technical resources necessary to bring the program together. Rich had been involved in many of the Skunk Works' famous projects, and the authors feel that it is fitting that this book be dedicated to his efforts.

Actual F-117 Flight Testing
During the initial phase of F-117 flight testing, the F-117 was not used at all. The venerable A-7 fighter, a plane that was on its way out of the inventory, was used to simulate the F-117 flying characteristics. In fact, initial personnel in the program were told that they would be running avionics tests and evaluations for the A-7 weapon system. Needless to say, there was some doubt that this was the real mission, since nobody could figure out why such secrecy would be employed on such an old aircraft.

Again, the security of the program was vigorous during those early days and throughout the program. A number of rumors circulated about the existence of an advanced stealth fighter, but its existence sure couldn't have been confirmed. It was still a heavy secret.

The pilot selection process was perhaps the most rigorous portion of the program. The pilots selected were truly the best of the 'Top Guns', "skimmed off the top" based on their records. It must be remembered that before the establishment of an F-117 simulator in 1986, every first flight for these pilots was a solo.

F-117 pilot John Zink recalled the circumstances in his selection for the program. "They said they couldn't tell me very much about what I was going to be doing, but that it was certainly in the national interest. That's how the invitation came for an F-117 assignment."

As with the development of any current program, cost was a prime consideration with the F-117, too. To that end, as many off-the-shelf components as possible were utilized.

A 37th Tactical Fighter Wing F-117A at the 1991 DOD Joint Services Open House at Andrews AFB, MD. (DOD Photo)

The GE F404 powerplants were the same as those utilized on the Navy F/A-l8, while the USAF F-16 and F/A-18 donated certain cockpit equipment. Certain navigation electronics even came from the venerable B-52 bomber. Environmental control systems came from the C-130, and the flight control computers were extracted from the F-16.

There were a total of five airframes constructed for the flight test program. The first pair were used to demonstrate basic flight characteristics.

Project officials had hoped that the first flight would take place in July 1980, but it was not until January of the following year that the F-117 craft (tail number 780) would be delivered. It would be eleven months later, in June 1981, that the 780 test bird would finally take to the air. By the way, those early F-117s were painted gray.

It did not take long for Lockheed engineers to determine that the vertical tails were too small for adequate aircraft stability. The problem was solved by doubling the area of the rudders.

Because of the aircraft's shaping, it was necessary to develop new control laws for implementation in the flight control system. In addition, new interfaces for the new air data sensors and a redundant data management system were developed.

Other problems faced during the flight test program were basically concentrated in the combination of tailpipe and hot gas flow areas. The nozzle is a 2D rectangular design and a design nightmare. There are inner and outer exposed surfaces in the tailpipe which caused stresses when the engine was started. To solve the problem, it was necessary to run up the engines before the taxi out in order to equalize the two structures.

The second heating problem came from hot exhaust leaks into the aft deck. With the complex stealth shaping, it was almost impossible to promote secondary flow. The F-117 had some very tough engineering problems to be solved, that's for sure.

Early in the flight test program, there was concern about high angle-of-attack flight. The worry came from the fact that wind tunnel model studies had indicated a potential problem. For that reason, the pilots used the simulator extensively before attempting such maneuvers in actual flight.

Since air refueling was an important part of the ultimate F-117 mission, it was also important in the flight test program. The handling qualities of the F-117 proved to be excellent in moving up to and pulling back from the tanker. The F-117 was very stable under the tanker; indeed, test pilots commented that they felt that they could take their hands off the controls for a short period and still remain in position. However, there were problems locating the tanker in night-time conditions without radar.

The first test aircraft to carry a weapon system was the number three bird (Number 782). The plane quickly proved the effectiveness of the delivery system when the weapon was placed directly on the target area. Weapon separation testing required an extensive modification to the airframe. In order to handle the 2000 bombs, it was necessary to extensively beef up the weapons trapeze.

The precision of the delivery continued to be improved, with the CEP well within tolerances. When the program was initiated, there were plans for a wide variation of weapons to be carried and delivered by the F-117. But in the end, the weapon suite would be very modest.

Besides proving the airworthiness of the airframe design, the test program also had the ambitious goal of proving the Radar Cross Section (RCS) capabilities of the design. The actual stealth demonstration aircraft was Number 783, the first model to receive the "stealth coating." That first covering presented initial problems which were worked out before the technique was applied to the production versions. The RCS testing was accomplished completely at night.

Like other new aircraft, the F-117 test program also included heat and icing tests along with wet runway testing. Fortunately, the new coating proved capable of withstanding the environmental forces.

One of the scariest moments in the test program took place when Number 785, the first production version, lost control on takeoff. The aircraft crashed back to earth, causing major damage to the front of the craft. Fortunately, the pilot was rescued from the burning craft. Number 785 never flew again, but was subsequently used by Lockheed as a mock-up for the fitting of new components.

On another occasion, an F-117 was flying a high-speed test when a rudder blew off the aircraft. The test pilot was informed about the potentially-dangerous situation, but was able to land the plane safely.

Following the announcement of the F-117 configuration in 1988, much of the flying started taking place during daylight hours. As a result, a public audience began to view the strange new planes. During 1989, for example, as many as ten aircraft were sighted over populated areas near Edwards Air Force Base. There were a number of close calls in the test program, but the skill of the test team and test pilots averted many potential disasters. As such, the F-117 was able to make it to IOC status in only two years and four months. In all, the program involved almost 500 sorties, far short of the originally-planned 850. There were 721 total flight test hours, with a maximum of 620 personnel working on the program.

Production

So far, we have called the aircraft the F-117, which is not quite correct. When the plane entered production status, it carried the more official name of F-117A, indicating this was the first variation of the Blackhawk built. Whether there will ever be a second version remains to be seen. In the mid-1990s, that didn't seem very likely.

The first production aircraft was the aforementioned number 785, which was lost in the crash on April 20, 1982. Number 786 was then accepted on September 2, 1982. Thereafter, the planes followed with consecutive numbering. Number 843 was the final craft, delivered in July 1990.

With the delivery of the fifteenth production aircraft (Number 799), the 4450th Test Group, which ran the test program, was declared operational.

The initial twenty production aircraft were produced at a ten-per-year rate with follow-on production dropping off to eight per year. Completion of the production phase of the F-117 program was accomplished more than two months ahead of schedule.

The total production for the F-117A was 59 (along with the five flight test versions) with the final production plane being accepted by the Air Force on July 13, 1990. The formal ceremony was held at Lockheed's Plant 10 in Palmdale, California. General Michael Dugan, then the Air Force Chief of Staff, accepted the plane from Lockheed officials.

In his keynote speech, General Dugan explained, "The F-117 program is a model of success . . . on cost, on schedule, and on performance."

The average unit flyaway cost per aircraft was $42.6 million, which included all government-furnished equipment. This relatively low cost was achieved even though the F-117 had an extremely low production rate. The cost compared favorably to that of other fighters with production rates more than ten times as high."

In line with the high security nature of the program throughout its years, the F-117 received its own unique series of serial numbers. The three-digit identification numbers varied from the normal USAF numbering sequence in that they didn't carry the year of production in front of them, i.e. 83-780.

Although the term 'series production' would generally indicate a number of identical aircraft, that was not the case with the F-117A.

Each of the aircraft was slightly different from the preceding model. Different innovations were incorporated as they became available, such as a new type of digital moving map, color multifunction displays, etc. The earlier models would later be retrofitted with the additions.

Table 1: Complete Production Chronology for the F-117

Production	Serial	Acceptance date
FSD	780	Not available
FSD	781	Not available
FSD	782	Not available
FSD	783	Not available
FSD	784	Not available
1	785	Lost before acceptance
2	786	Sept. 2, 1982
3	787	Aug. 23, 1982
4	788	Oct. 22, 1982
5	789	Nov. 17. 1982
6	790	Dec. 11, 1982
7	791	Dec. 13, 1982
8	792	Dec. 22, 1982
9	793	Feb. 1, 1983
10	794	April 15, 1983
11	795	Sept. 9, 1983
12	796	Aug. 4, 1983
13	797	Aug. 31, 1983
14	798	Oct. 3, 1983
15	799	Oct. 28, 1983
16	800	Dect. 7, 1983
17	801	Feb. 15, 1984
18	802	April 6, 1984
19	803	June 22, 1984
20	804	June 20, 1984
21	805	Aug. 3, 1984
22	806	Sept. 12, 1984
23	807	Nov. 28, 1984
24	808	Dec. 20, 1984
25	809	April 16, 1985
26	810	Feb. 14, 1985
27	811	March 29, 1985
28	812	June 12, 1985
29	813	July 10, 1985
30	814	Sept. 5, 1985
31	815	Oct. 31, 1985
32	816	Dec. 20, 1985
33	817	Feb. 28, 1986
34	818	May 22, 1986
35	819	April 24, 1986
36	820	June 19, 1986
37	821	Aug. 1, 1986
38	822	Sept. 18, 1986
39	823	Dec. 4, 1986
40	824	Dec. 17, 1986
41	825	March 25, 1987
42	826	March 25, 1987
43	827	May 18,1987
44	828	June 17, 1987
45	829	Nov. 27, 1987
46	830	Nov. 27, 1987
47	831	Nov. 27, 1987
48	832	Feb. 11, 1988
49	833	May 25, 1988
50	834	May 27, 1988
51	835	Aug. 15, 1988
52	836	Oct. 19,1988
53	837	Feb. 22, 1989
54	838	May 24, 1989
55	839	Aug. 14, 1989
56	840	Nov. 1, 1989
57	841	March 8, 1989
58	842	March 28, 1990
59	843	July 1990

Note: The FSD through production model number 15 carried the 700 series numbering, while the remainder of the 59 production aircraft were numbered with 800 series numbers. (USAF Chart)

High-ranking U.S. Air Force and Lockheed officials pose in front of the F-117A Stealth Fighter–59th and final aircraft in the current program—in July 12 ceremonies at Palmdale, California. Left to right are Ben Rich, president of Lockheed Advanced Development Company, which developed and built the Stealth Fighters; Gen. Michael Dugan, USAF chief of staff; Dan Tellep, Lockheed Corporation chairman and chief executive officer; and Paul Martin, Lockheed F-117A program manager. Lockheed delivered the first F-17A in 1982. The final F-117A was delivered July 12, 1990, at the Palmdale ceremonies.

Chapter Three
Nighthawk Parts and Pieces

The F-117 Nighthawk, the first Air Force fighter aircraft designed to cruise virtually undetected by radar and infrared sensor systems, doesn't look like any other airplane. Its flat, black, faceted surface reflects little visually. And its appearance—even in flight—is that of something alien, of something which doesn't belong.

The Nighthawk weighs 52,500 pounds and is roughly the size of an F-15. Its length is just under 66 feet, wingspan is 43 feet, four inches, and height is about twelve-and-a-half feet. The wings are swept back 67.5 degrees. While the F-15 Eagle has what could be called gracefully flowing lines, the F-117 is a pile of trapezoidal shapes. Where the Eagle's wings and tail "naturally" flow into its fuselage, the Nighthawk's wings and other pieces are jammed into its middle.

Perhaps the most unusual—or even disturbing—aspect of the mostly aluminum alloy F-117's appearance is the illusion that the aircraft changes shape significantly as the viewer walks around it. For example, in the view of it offered by the grainy, black and white picture released by the Air Force in 1988 from the front just off starboard, the aircraft appears to be short and stocky. If one continued around the wing toward the tail, the aircraft would elongate into a surprisingly long and thin rear fuselage, and the swallow-tail fins, each of which pivots on a center pin, sweep back dramatically.

The odd facets are there to control as much as possible the reflection of radar beams. Curved surfaces scatter beams in several directions, thus making radar returns possible. The F-117's surfaces are arranged so that radar beams are re-flected off in directions away from radars. These features include sharp facet intersections which are similarly angled to reduce radar returns. If one looks closely at the Nighthawk, he'd see sawtooth edges on access panels, on cockpit/fuselage intersections, and on the two bomb bay doors. Every facet is angled at least 30 degrees from the vertical.

Other important stealth design features include engine inlet grills on either side of the forward fuselage area which shield engine compressor stage blades from prying radars. On the aft end of the fuselage in the shape of thin, horizontal slits stretching from the inner wing trailing edges to the base of the tails, the outlets serve dual purposes: again, reducing radar detection; and minimizing the aircraft's infrared signature by causing the exhaust plume to rapidly dissipate.

A pair of modified General Electric engines, designated F404-F1D2, power the Nighthawk. Each of these non-afterburning engines is made to minimize smoke. Also, each has a wide fan to mix cool air from the nozzle with the hot air from the engine core; this cooling and the fact that the Nighthawk flies subsonic keeps the infrared signature to a minimum. Having a thrust-to-weight ratio of six-to-one, the F404 originally was developed as an afterburning engine for the U.S. Navy F/A-18 fighter. The F1D2 modifications saved weight savings and maintained enough power to make the F-117 a very high subsonic speed aircraft.

The F-117's sharp surface facets required careful design so as not to incur performance penalties. The facets cause

The changing faces of the F-117. Look at the F-117 straight on and level, and it doesn't even resemble an aircraft as we know it. Move up closer and slightly under, looking up, and suddenly the wings sweep back and a pyramid appears, changing the total appearance of the plane. (USAF Photo)

Looking at the F-117 from a high-left-rear view, the aircraft looks different yet again. Since the F-117 is made up not of various parts that flow smoothly into each other, but rather of oddly-shaped triangles, trapezoids, and parallelograms, each perspective appears totally different. (USAF Photo)

vortices to form when the aircraft is in motion and these vortices tend to complement the overall airflow around the aircraft. They not only help maintain lift and reduce drag, but also direct airflow into the engine inlets.

The Nighthawk's F-16-like, quadruple-redundant fly-by-wire controls, combined with a state-of-the-art digital avionics suite and automated mission planning system, keep the aircraft flying nicely.

To remain stealthy, the Nighthawk can carry nothing externally, including fuel tanks. It relies upon aerial refueling for long range flights. Its ordnance load of two 2,000 pound GBU-27 laser-guided bombs hang inside twin bomb bay compartments on trapeze racks resembling wishbone automobile suspension members turned vertical. When the bombs are ready to be dropped they are electronically activated, the bomb bay doors open, and each bomb swings down on its trapeze carriage and is released (some sources cite the F-117's capability of carrying the AGM-65 Maverick or AGM-88

Modern fighters by definition are sleek aerodynamic machines without that first sharp corner. But check out this view of the F-117, which appears to violate every rule of modern fighter design. Note particularly the large angle change between the canopy and rear fuselage. (USAF Photo)

An interesting comparision of tails. The normal T-tail configuration of a standard heavy transport is in stark contrast to the 'V' configuration of the F-117. (John Farquhar Photo)

HARM air-to-surface missiles, as well as the AIM-9 Sidewinder air-to-air missile).

The windscreen consists of five segments, giving the pilot enough visibility to the front and sides to land and take off. The windscreen material itself is very nonreflective of light and may contain some radar absorbent material.

Radar absorbent material covers wing leading edges and parts of the forward fuselage. Also, it is believed that the aircraft paint is radar absorbent. Trailing edge parts are made of a new kind of resin which is not only damage-resistant, but also very tolerant of high temperatures. Design and material features have resulted in an aircraft which has an RCS of probably that of a small bird or less.

Business for the F-117 Nighthawk is attacking ground targets at night. A FLIR, or Forward-Looking InfraRed sensor, is one of the pieces of equipment which enables the aircraft to carry out its missions. FLIRs produce clear images to

The F-117A V-tail fin pivots on a center pin. (Wallace Drawing)

The F-117 presents a collection of unusual angles. A good example can be found when viewing the Nighthawk from the side. Notice the extreme slant of the rear twin tails from the sloping fuselage. There has never been anything like it in aeronautical history. (John Farquhar Photo)

Looking closely at the F-I17 tail, which features a movable flight control surface, a crease line can be noted which aids the aircraft's stealthiness. This plane also carries the 37th Tactical Fighter Wing logo. (John Farquhar Photo)

Sitting on the ground, the nose wheel door shows the same kind of zig-zag pattern as other parts of the aircraft, such as the cockpit windows. Also notice the engine inlet grills located just above the wing. (John Farquhar Photo)

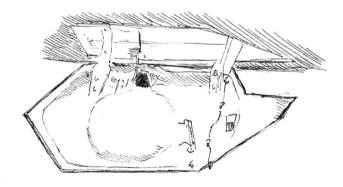

The inner surface of the landing gear door is painted white. (Wallace Drawing)

Stealth does not continue to the F-117 nose gear, which is a pretty conventional unit. After all, it's not going to be in its extended position in the heat of combat. (John Farquhar Photo)

the pilot and, since they do not radiate like radars, they cannot be detected. Their limitation, compared to radar, is a relatively narrow field-of-view likened to "searching for a target while looking through a straw."

To overcome this limitation, the FLIR is used in conjunction with an inertial navigation system (INS) which "keeps track" of every acceleration, deceleration, pitch, roll, etc., of the aircraft and computes present position. Although the modern INS is not perfect, it is accurate to within a few hundred yards or less and operational experience has demonstrated its adequacy.

The F-117's FLIR sensor is just ahead and below the front windscreen, and sits behind a RAM-coated screen. It has both (relatively) wide and narrow field-of-view settings. There is also a downward-looking infrared (DLIR) sensor mounted under the fuselage which has a laser designator.

The pilot locates his target using the FLIR/INS, attacks it using the laser designator and precision munitions, and leaves the scene. The laser designator and DLIR remain trained on the target to ensure a very high probability of success. The GBU-27 bomb, by virtue of its on-board electronics, controls the direction of its descent towards the area designated by the laser.

Inside the cockpit, the pilot gets the information he needs to navigate and carry out his mission primarily by means of a large cathode ray tube, multifunction display. There are also smaller multifunction displays on each side of the central CRT which provide the pilot with the status of aircraft systems, communications, and weapons.

A majority of the F-117's weight is supported more-of-less conventionally by the twin gears extending down from the extremely wide fuselage. Long and spindly, these gears give the F-117 the look of an insect when it is sitting on the ground. (John Farquhar Photo)

Like the fictional 'Invisibile Man', the F-117 can wreak havoc upon unsuspecting targets. (USAF Photo)

The past, present, and future are depicted by this shot at the U.S. International Air and Trade Show. The past is represented by the F-4 Phantom, the present with the Navy F/A-18, with the F-117 showing the way of the future. (USAF Photo)

At the pilot's left hand is the parachute deployment handle. Interestingly, F-117 landings are nearly always made with parachute aid for slowing the aircraft on the runway.

Completing the picture is the McDonnell Douglas Aces II ejection seat, a U.S. military aircraft standard. However, some parts of this seat are painted for F-117-specific use to avoid the possibility of any glint off the metal.

The F-117 Nighthawk made use of as much "off-the-shelf" equipment as possible for cost effectiveness, but the end product is certainly unique and, as we shall see in the next chapter, a deadly tool in the hands of USAF pilots.

With the canopy in the open position, the head-up display and a portion of the ACES II Ejection Seat are visible. Directly in front of the canopy joining point is the homeplate-shaped, forward-looking infrared turret. (USAF Photo)

(Wallace Drawing)

This detail of the enclosed cockpit area shows the characteristic radar-jumbling zig-zag design of the F-117 canopy. Also note the peculiar point atop the canopy. Daytime visibility was not a prime design consideration since the stealth fighter's world is one of darkness. (John Farquhar Photo)

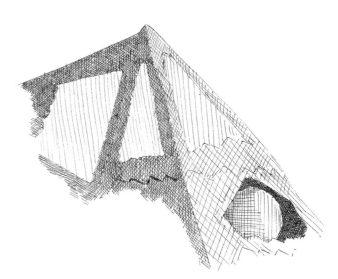

Directly in front of the cockpit is the Forward Looking Infrared Sensor. (Wallace Drawing)

Another example of how a change in the viewing angle of the F-117 seems to present a completely different machine. From one viewpoint the aircraft seems to have a somewhat stubby shape, while from another the airplane seems to elongate all out of expected proportion. (John Farquhar Photo)

A pilot sits in an F-117 simulator. Visible on the top is the aircraft's head-up display. Immediately below is a panel giving navigation, speed, altitude, and other data. The square screen directly beneath is the infrared display, sitting directly between two multifunction displays which can provide many types of information, including moving maps for precise navigation at night. The handle at bottom center is the ejection seat activator. (USAF Photo)

Notice the opening directly above the engine intakes, shown here open on the ground.

Although not readily apparent, the cockpit glass is non-reflective. This keeps it in line with the opaque, low-observable look of the aircraft. (UASF Photo)

A look inside the bomb bay of the Nighthawk. This portside view shows the 2000-pound bomb mounting mechanism and details of the bomb attachment mechanism. (Spencer P. Lane Photo)

Looking forward through the bomb bay, the wishbone hanger on which the bomb is hung is in the 'down' position. The fins of the bomb are visible at the bottom of the photo. (Spencer P. Lane Photo)

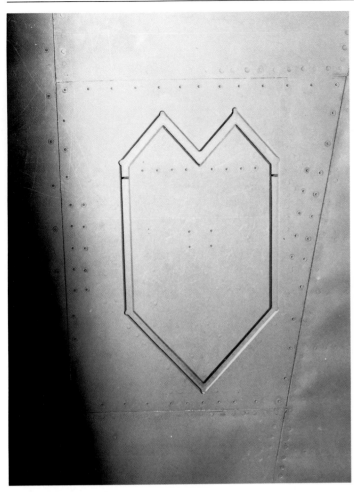

The other end of the F-117 propulsion system is shown with this view of the exhaust outlet. The design shields the exhaust from infrared sensors, but still allows adequate thrust from the GE F404 engine to propel the aircraft. (Spencer P. Lane Photo)

The sawtooth pattern, for radar deflection, is in evidence everywhere, even on this fuselage access panel. (Spencer P. Lane Photo)

Looking up at the portside engine inlet grill, which carries a type of screening. This screening is just another device to hide the engine and aid in radar signature reduction. (Spencer P. Lane Photo)

The split flat arrangement on the trailing edge of the left wing is shown. The bright USAF rondell, shown on this pre-production aircraft on display in the Air Force Museum, was not carried through to the operational versions. (Spencer P. Lane Photo)

Chapter Four
The F-117 Goes to War

Never in the history of modern American fighter aircraft has a plane been called upon to go to combat so quickly after its development. The F-117 first tasted combat in a stike in Panama in 1989.

However, the aircraft had also come very close to seeing combat four years earlier. In mid-1986, a pair of F-117s had been armed to participate in a pair of highly-clasdified missions. The exact target to be hit was never been officially identified, but just hours before take-off, the mission was strangely cancelled.

During the years to follow, several F-117s were kept on alert. As such, these particular planes did not participate in the training exercises that were being carried out at the time.

With the surgical strike capabilities of the F-117, there were many interesting mission scenarios considered for the aircraft. These missions would not have been possible before

In an era of Mach Two fighters, glowing afterburners, blazing Gatling guns, and air-to-air missiles, this strange black bat did its job quietly, almost invisibly. It was one of the stars of Desert Storm. (USAF Photo)

The view from the boom operater of a tanker while it refuels an F-117. Note the location of the refueling receptacle just aft of the cockpit. (USAF Photo)

Like its contemporaries, the F-117 used its aerial refueling capabilities to carry out its combat missions. (USAF Photo)

Nothing has ever looked like this swarm of wasp-like machines shown here, as almost two dozen F-117s await their next mission. (USAF Photo)

Although the F-117's first combat mission was during Operation Just Cause in Panama, it became a star during Desert Storm. (USAF Photo)

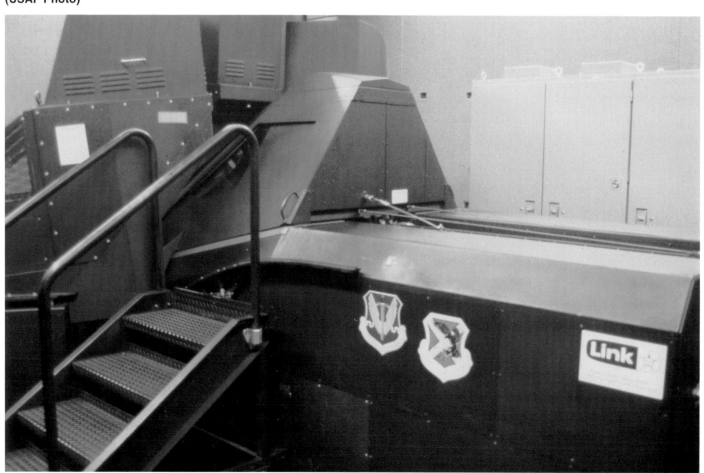

Since the first flight for any F-117 pilot was (and is) a solo, ground simulation was a necessity. Considering that the initial flying was also done completely at night, and the importance of this simulator can't be overstated. (USAF Photo)

Another view of the F-117 simulator, with the "cockpit" pushed into the simulation position. (USAF Photo)

As can be seen, attack from the air was not a serious consideration as seen by the close-in staging. (USAF Photo)

this magnificent aircraft arrived on the scene. Of particular interest were counterinsurgency missions, in which munitions are quickly and silently placed on a target area.

It was thought at the time that with its unique mission capabilities, the F-117 might not fit in with the more standard operational aircraft of the then-Tactical Air Command. Debate over the capabilities of the F-117 and how it would actually be deployed could have been a reason that the initial buy of some one hundred aircraft was reduced to only 59.

As was stated earlier, the initial operational F-117 unit carried the designation of the 4450th TG, a unit that was activated in October 1989. Later, the organization was renamed the 37th Fighter Group. Within the group were the 415th and 416th Tactical Fighter Squadrons. The 417th TFS was the designation given to the training squadron of the group.

F-117 training within the 4450th was vigorous, and considerable target practice was carried out. On some nights,

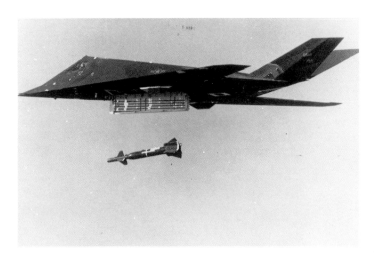

Sadam Hussein's worst nightmare: an invisible airplane and an ultra-precision laser-guided bomb. (USAF Photo)

there were numerous targets located and identified on the test range. The winner of these competitions was determined by evaluation of videotapes. A portion of the testing was also carried out at ranges at both the Nellis and Edwards Air Force Bases.

Since aerial refueling was expected to be a part of the actual missions for the F-117, that operation was included in the training program. An interesting offshoot of this training was the fact that boom operators were also trained on the differences of refueling this strange new plane. That tricky operation was usually accomplished in the complete black of night, certainly a challenging situation.

Surprisingly, according to a number of F-117 pilots, the cubical black machine really doesn't fly that much different from a 'normal aircraft.' The similarity is caused basically from the fact that the F-117's computerized flight control system was taken from the F-16. Even so, the F-117 got a bad rap in the

Protection was a high priority with the F-117 during Desert Storm. This photo shows the single-plane bunkers where the F-117s resided while on the ground. (USAF Photo)

This F-117 is receiving maintainance alongside service facilities in Saudi Arabia. (USAF Photo)

A night fighter at night. This Nighthawk is getting ready for an evening run to downtown Baghdad. In all, the F-117s dropped two thousand tons of bombs and hit 40 percent of the total targets attacked by Allied aircraft. (USAF Photo)

press for alleged handling problems. There was even a name given to it, "Wobblin' Goblin", for those supposed bad tendancies.

Most of the plane's pilots, though, would certainly argue with that evaluation. Pilots indicated that many called it the "Black Jet" with a feeling of great affection.

"The visibility isn't great," one pilot conceeded. That's easy to understand, though, because of the cockpit location which sits right above the chiseled-appearing nose. Recall again that instead of the normal bubble canopy, the pilot has only five flat windows, one on each side and three forward.

In 1989, the F-117 finally participated in an action for its intended design purpose, the precise placing of munitions on a target. The mission was a strike in Panama against a Panamanian Defense Forces installation at Rio Hato during the American invasion of the country. The location was home to the Panama Defense Forces 6th and 7th infrantry companies, and also the location of General Manuel Noriega's home.

The attack is reported to have involved six F-117s attacking in pairs with 2,000-pound bombs equipped with time-delay fuzes. According to Defense Department officials, the

Sketch of infrared target, with cross hairs centered, as seen by F-117 pilots during Desert Storm in 1990. The same pictures were available to U.S. televsion viewers throughout the war. (Wallace drawing)

Because of the overwhelming success of the U.S. air effort and the destruction of the Iraqi Air Force in only a few days, it was possible to carry out maintenance in broad daylight. (USAF Photo)

Coming in from a mission, this F-117 deploys its drag chute upon touchdown. (USAF Photo)

Although it was central to the war, the F-117 never felt the wrath of battle; no Nighthawk got a single bullet hole. (USAF Photo)

The F-111 was another key player in Desert Storm, making many bomb runs. Since it is not a stealthy aircraft like the F-117, it was much more vulnerable to ground fire. (USAF Photo)

Due to the low-humidity desert environemt, the F-117's infrared sensors could operate at their peak. (USAF Photo)

It is a tall first step up to the cockpit for either the pilot or the maintenance technician. The four-section unit is clearly visible in this photo. (USAF Photo)

purpose of the operation was to "Disorient, stun and confuse" the Panamanian troops in the area. Minutes after the strike, the infantrymen scattered and were in a state of disarray. Many fled and several hundred were taken prisoner.

The Rio Hato mission was the only one flown by the F-117s, but it was officially stated that other missions had been considered, but were cancelled.

For an operation that could easily have been accomplished by existing operational aircraft, there was some question as to why the F-117 was used. Uncertainty, though, about the level of air defense at the installation was the main reasoning to use this aircraft. The head of an engineering firm in Panama said that he was astonished to learn that the F-117 was used in this relatively simple mission.

It would later be reported that a number of the F-117-delivered weapons were significantly off target, and the new stealth fighter caught a lot of the blame. It wasn't the debut that the Air Force had hoped for!

Following the Panama mission, the F-117 gained more exposure when the 37th TFW was moved from its Groom Lake desert location to Holloman Air Force Base, New Mexico, where it assumed the location of a former T-38 unit. In order to accomodate the F-117s, it was necessary for some addi-

tional construction at the site. After all, the maintenance requirements for the F-117 are certainly eons different from those of the T-38.

With the experience acquired from the Panama operation, and the immediately-upcoming Desert Storm operation, the importance of the F-117 simulator became even more important. For the F-117 program, the simulator was(and is) one magnificent machine. The simulator is an essential training aid for F-117 pilots because when they step into their F-117 for the first time, that first flight will be a solo. Since the F-117 is only a single-seater, there is no instructor pilot in the back seat to aid the aviator in that first flight.

And then it came. Desert Storm and the F-117's chance to shine, which is something that it did with great success. As is well known, those significant accomplishments were carried on national TV. That little black stealthy machine was a new national hero!

The night of January l7, 1991, it started when F-117s performed the first Desert Storm mission, the placing of 2,000 pound bombs on the communications nerve center of the Iraqi Ministry of Defense in central Baghdad. The black birds swooped in undetected by the enemy radar systems, flying

The dark, menacing noses of these two Nighthawks are in stark contrast to the light Saudi desert. (USAF Photo)

As an F-117 gets towed to a maintenance area, Air Force technicians in the background take a well-deserved breather. (USAF Photo)

Another star of Desert Storm was this equally strange-looking plane, the A-10 Thunderbolt II, affectionately known as the Warthog. The A-10 proved especially adept at hitting trucks and tanks with its deadly 30mm Gatling gun and AGM-65 Maverick Missiles. (USAF Photo)

From this Desert Storm F-117, a multitude of shapes and shades cascade in the boiling desert sun. (USAF Photo)

It wasn't a complete USAF show in Desert Storm. Carrier-based F/A-I8D's like this one coordinated attacks with the F-117s for ultimate success. Note the Kuwaiti oil fields ablaze below. (McDonnell-Douglas Photo)

Part of the reason for the F-117's success was due to the air superiority gained from F-16s (on each end) and the F-15s (three in the middle). The near F-16, from Syracuse Air National Guard, was the first ANG unit to go to Desert Storm. The two darker F-15s are E Models from Seymour-Johnson Air Force Base. (USAF Photo)

The GBU-27 Laser Guided Bomb proved to be a lethal weapon during Desert Storm. Here, an F-117 dispenses its deadly load in test. In Desert Storm, though, all F-117 missions were carried out at night. (USAF Photo)

in from Khamis Mushait in Saudia Arabia, with mid-air refueling. During this first mission, there was no fighter support.

That was the first mission of six weeks of F-117 action as the Nighthawks continuously swooped out of the darkness of night, and performed their surgical dissection of Iraqi's military machine.

The chief of F-117 Desert Storm operations was Colonel Alton Whitley who had just taken command of the 37th TFW, a unit which in recent years has been renamed the 49th TFW, and whose planes carry an HO designation on the vertical tails.

The Colonel was certainly appropriate for the prestigious job as he was the first operational TAC pilot to fly the F-117, in October 1982.

Amazingly, only four hours into his new job, Colonel Whitley got orders to deploy to Saudi. Eventually, l8 F-117s would deploy to Saudi with KC-l0s providing petrol along the way. The desert setting of the King Khalid Air Base was very similar to the Tonopah Test Range. Those first planes came

Shown here is a loading operation of the GBU-27 Laser Guided Bomb, as it is maneuvered into its internal position. There are no wing-mounted weapons on the F-117, since they would obviously compromise the stealthiness of the aircraft. (Lockheed Photo)

from the 415th TFS with l8 additional aircraft coming later from the 416th.

The F-117 detachment was a part of the 335 attack aircraft deployed for Desert Storm. Other types included A-6, AV-8A, A-10 and F-111 aircraft. There were also 220 dual-role planes, including F-15s, F-16s, and Navy F/A-18s.

The new F-117 base on the desert quickly came together and after intensive training was completed, things were in

---

Desert Storm Combat by F-117 Pilot, Major Marcel Kerdavid

"Our target for that first mission(January 11, 1991) was the Khark Telecomminication Tower. We felt it was best to use a 10 milli-second delay to take out the antenna portion of the tower. We took off and flew 100 miles north to meet our tankers in radio silence. The tankers followed their lead to our pre-briefed drop-off point at the pre-briefed time. We then proceeded toward the target. I could see the lights still on in Baghdad from over a hundred miles away.

My systems all worked perfectly, and I armed my weapons delivery systems at the pre-IP(initial point). Inbound to the tower, I was totally focused on my target and photos. I found the tower and tracked the top as we had planned. When the weapon exploded and I finally looked up, I noted the sky was filled with AAA. It was so thick I swore I could have walked on it. I had to stay down in it until I hit my second target at the North Tiji military industrial complex.

I was relieved to hear all the flights were checking in at the tankers with no losses. The cruise home seemed to take forever. I couldn't wait to get back, talk to all the other players, and review my tape."

F-117s sit in front of their reinforced concrete hangers in Saudi Arabia. (USAF Photo)

Desert Storm Combat by F-117 Pilot, Captain Rob Donaldson

"All my F-117 missions were memorable, but the one that was the most satisfying was on the last night of the war. My wingman that night was Major Lee Gustin and our target was Party Headquarters in downtown Baghdad. It was a motivating mission because the organization was headed by Saddam.

My machine was loaded with two two-thousand pound bombs. Then I taxied out onto the runway and we took off in 20 second intervals. We flew for an hour and hooked up with our KC-l35 tanker. We then went on separate routes and I headed north.

My route took me south of Baghdad, around to the northest and then southwest across the city. As I approached the city, I saw a brilliant flash on the ground which looked like a SAM missile launch. It passed about a quarter mile off my right side, close enough to hear the rocket motor.

I then turned to my final attack heading, descended even lower, and picked up more speed. Timing was critical because all the other F-117s out there were counting on me being on the attitude and on time just as I was trusting them to do the same. I acquired my assigned target and put the cross-hairs over the specific corner of the building. I released both bombs at once and kept the laser beam right on target.

Just as my bombs hit, many other bombs from the other F-117s exploded into the entire building complex. Up until that point, not a shot had been fired. The Iraqis were completely surprised, but as soon as the bombs went off, they started shooting. It looked like the best fourth of July fireworks display. Tracers and missiles were going off all over the place.

We had to fly through all that stuff, yet miraculously, not a single F-117 took a hit during the entire course of the war.

I got out of Baghdad as fast as the jet would go and joined up with Lee back at the border. We then called the AWACS to tell them we were coming across. Then, after refueling from the same tanker, we cruised the 600 miles back to base.

I was tired, but was awakened the next morning by a bunch of hooting and hollering. I got up and was told that the second wave of F-117s had been turned back because the war was over!

My mission proved to be the last F-117 mission of the war and I was proud to be a part of it. I want to personally thank all the crew chiefs, bomb loaders, and other support people whose dedication and attention to detail enabled me and my fellow F-117 pilots to perform so effectively during the war.

They are the true heros of Team Stealth."

A U.S. soldier inspects damage at an enemy facility. Bombs like the GBU-27, carried by the F-117, could inflict serious damage with pinpoint accuracy. This surgical precision enabled U.S. forces to hit military targets without causing civilian casualties. (USAF Photo)

Advanced technology helped the U.S. and its allies win Operation Desert Storm. U.S. combat aircraft like the F-117 hit tanks, bridges, bunkers, chemical production plants, and weapon storage facilities with marked effect. Their effectiveness was documented in photographs like this for damage assessment teams. (Department of Defense Photo)

place. The goal was to be ready when the UN deadline of January 15, 1991 came due.

There was no waiting for a second chance when the time came and went and the Iraqi's had not withdrawn. It came just before midnight on the night of January 16th. The base was filled with the whine of jet engines as the F-117s began to appear from their hardened silos. It wouldn't be until the wee hours of the following morn-ing (actually 2:51AM) that the black birds took to the night skies for the aforementioned first mission.

The 415th planes led the attack, followed shortly thereaf-ter by 416th aircraft. The enemy never knew what hit him as the attack was completely undetected by the Iraqis. Report-edly, the lights of Baghad were still on even when the attack was underway. The weapons of choice this night included various versions of Paveway laser guided bombs.

The secrecy of the raid and the effectiveness of the plane were aptly demonstrated by the fact that there were some three thousand AAA guns and 60 surface-to-air missiles in place to protect the Baghdad area, with none finding their mark on any of the F-117s.

The second F-117 raid was carried out with eight aircraft carrying laser-guided bombs, with similar success. It came on January 26th with the target list being expanded to in-clude the likes of aircraft facilities, bridges, and storage sites. It was considered that on some of these very heavily-defended facilities the Nighthawks would have a better chance of sur-vival. They did! Although the action from the F-117s during

Even though it is not a high-performance aircraft like the F-15 or F-16, there is still the need for a drag parachute. (USAF Photo)

the short conflict recieved a tremendous barrage of positive publicity, it must be confessed that actually only about 2.5 percent of the total action involved the F-ll7 operations. But when the F-117 target hits were shown nightly in the U.S. on national TV, it was hard indeed not to make the Blackhawk a hero!

Specific F-117 targets targeted in downtown Baghdad included command and control buildings, communications centers, and radar facilities.   Of course, as is remembered, the night skies were filled with AAA fire attempting to bring down the F-117s and other allied aircraft during their missions

An Air Force technician performs maintenance on an F-117A prior to a mission. (USAF Photo)

In addition to bunkers and other fortified structures, U.S. forces in Desert Storm went after armored vehicles with the same deadly results. (USAF Photo)

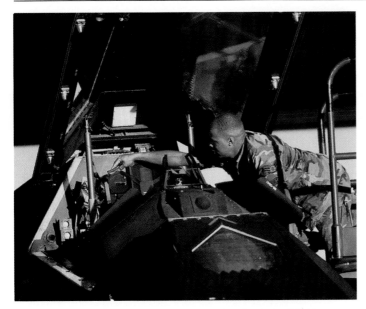

A Maintenance NCO pulls an electronic check inside the cockpit of an F-117A. (USAF Photo)

Captain Jack Shepherd awaits the signal from a ground crewman before rolling into position for take-off. (USAF Photo)

over the capital city, but the F-117s didn't get so much as a single bullet hole during the whole Desert Storm operation. Throughout the war, Iraqi gunners were just hoping that a one-chance-in-a-million would take place and they could bring down one of the black fighters.

In discussing F-117 operations during the war, one F-117 pilot reported that when you started electronic jamming prior to an incoming mission, you tipped your hand that something is about to take place. It was noted that the Iraqi's would fill the sky with AAA fire immediately when jamming began. The F-117 pilots stated that they would just as soon use surprise

as their pat hand and go in quickly, do their job, and then get the heck out.

Four days after the start of the conflict, 17 F-117s struck oil pipelines around the Iraqi capital with almost magic efficiency, destroying 32 of 34 targets attacked.

Desert Storm air commander Lt. General Horner pointed to the flexibility of the F-117 in the conflict. He noted that the command found some F-117 fighters that had been programmed for a specific mission, were also given the rough coordinates for other targets and then diverted them to attack enemy aircraft on the ground. Horner indicated that six

There's nothing like dropping your whole load in one swoop, as this F-117A is doing in a test. Although each is armed with only two smart bombs, the F-117s hit close to 100 percent of their assigned targets, which accounted for about 40 percent of all the allies targets of the war. (USAF Photo)

In 1993, F-117As participated in TEAM SPIRIT exercises in South Korea, the first time that Nighthawks had ever been to that country. (USAF Photo)

After its great performance in Desert Storm, the F-117A was a great attraction at national air shows. Here it appears at the Dayton Air Show. (USAF Photo)

Lt. Col. Steven A. Green, 410th Test Squadron Commander at Edwards Air Force Base, is greeted by members of his unit after breaking the 1,000-hour milestone in the F-117A. The happy event took place in 1994. (USAF Photo)

A Nighthawk from the 37th Tactical Fighter Wing, Tonopah Test Range, Nevada, is landing for an overnight stay while deploying to Saudi Arabia during Operation Desert Shield, April 1992. (USAF Photo)

The serene orange glow of the sunset is in stark contrast to the sinister silhouette of an F-117A undergoing maintenance. (USAF Photo)

of those aircraft were destroyed on the ground before they could be launched against the allied fleet.

Now, here are some extremely interesting facts about the overall F-117 accomplishments in the six-week conflict. In all, the Nighthawks dropped over two thousand tons of ordnance on the target and actually hit some 40 percent of the total targets. In all, there were 1,270 missions flown by the F-117's.

It was advertised at the time that a majority of the F-117 missions were carried out alone without the normal escorts. Normally, bombing aircraft would have been supported by a number of radar-jamming aircraft, aircraft such as the F-4G Wild Weasels and EA-6Bs.

Later though, Air Force officials would admit that the F-117s did receive some electronic support that had earlier been denied. Even still, those same officials indicated that they thought the F-117s could have still accomplished the effort on their own. The point continued to be made ,though, that to accomplish their missions, the F-117s did not require the extensive airborne support package such that is required by conventional fighters.

Surprisingly, there were those that downgraded the contributions of the F-117 in the conflict. It was stated by some outside experts that the contributions of the F-117 were quite trivial. Guess that it's all in the eyes of the beholder in such evaluations.

In 1994, the F-117 would make the same trip again, back to the middle east. A dozen F-117s were included with B-52, A-10s, F-15s, F-16s, F-111s, AWACS, and other support aircraft that were sent to Saudi Arabia in the summer of that year when Saddam again moved troops to the Kuwaiti border.

At press time, the Nighthawks had not dropped a bomb (can't say fired a shot since the F-117 doesn't carry a gun) in anger. It was being reported at the time that many of these planes could be permanently stationed over there. It was also being considered at press time to deploy F-117s to Bosnia. Earlier, the Italians (it was reported) had placed a request to base the planes in that country.

To give the idea that the F-117 has been around for some time, you might be surprised that the first pilot-Lt. Col Steven Green-commander of the 4l0th Flight Test Squadron at Edwards Air Force Base became the first Nighthawk pilot to surpass one thousand hours in the F-117. Green indicated, "Of all the aircraft I've flown through the years, the F-117 is probably the best of them all."

As the F-117 matures, and its capabilities become better known, its use is changing in the late 1990s. The aircraft (instead of acting alone) is being integrated into strike packages as a special asset.

Chapter Five
The Future of the F-117

With the huge success of the F-117 during its development, and its dramatic triumph during Desert Storm, the questions must be asked — what is in the future for this magnificent machine? Are there any modifications needed to make the plane more effective? These are certainly tough questions, and they can't be answered completely, but this chapter will address them as far as possible.

Without doubt, the turndown in military spending in the 1990s will effect the construction of any new stealth aircraft, or any continuation of F-117 production. During the mid-1990s, though, stealth is still alive and well. The stealthy F-22 is nearing series production, a continuation of the B-2 stealth bomber is being deliberated, and the new JAST fighter is on the horizon.

During the late 1980s, it appeared that the replacement for the F-117 would be manifested in the form of the Navy's Advanced Tactical Aircraft, to be constructed by General Dynamics and McDonnell Douglas. Using an advanced level of stealth technologies, the so-called A-12 was to have used GE F404 powerplants, similar to those used for the F-117. Differences in the A-12 aircraft, though, were in the weapons capability, which greatly improved upon that of the F-117. The bomb load was estimated to be more like that of the F-111 or A-6. The A-12 also incorporated a high-resolution radar, two-man crew, and high-tech cockpit displays.

USAF, at the time, estimated that the A-12 might be able to replace or supplement the F-117 fleet. But in 1990, the USAF purchase of any A-12s was put off until 1997. Then, in the early 1990s, the program was cancelled completely, negating any of those possibilities.

In 1991, a $140 million appropriation was authorized to begin research into a so-called F-117A+ Derivative, involving the installation of the A-12 engine system into the F-117. According to the Air Force, the redesigned F-117 would see its combat range increased by 21 percent to almost 730 miles, along with a significant reduction of take-off roll. This project, however, did not happen either.

The possibility for renewed F-117 production also arose in 1991, when the British indicated an interest in purchasing a small number of the aircraft. Certainly, the performance of the F-117 in combat and Lockheed marketing stimulated their interest.

Although the purchase never took place, the UK Ministry of Defense was very serious about the purchase for a time.

In response to a Congressional request, Lockheed submitted a proposal indicating the circumstances for producing an additional forty aircraft. Lockheed indicated that the flyaway cost for the second batch of F-117s would be in the area of $43 million each, approximately $2.4 million more each than the initial USAF battery.

Although the proposed RAF version would have cost slightly more, it may have been well worth the expense, since a number of significant improvements were planned. Lockheed proposed redesigned engine inlets, a simpler exhaust system, and a bubble canopy (addressing the pilot visibility problems noted by F-117 pilots). It was stated at the time that those improvements could also have been retrofitted to the existing USAF fleet.

Lockheed also proposed an F-117N version, which was rejected by the Pentagon in mid-1993. The proposal was resubmitted with afterburning engines in 1994 to improve multi-role mission characteristics.

The N version of the F-117 was based on the F-117A, but carried a new wing with a 18 degree sweep with the capability of folding for shipboard stowage. The new design also included additional horizontal tail surfaces. The jet exhaust was modified along with new aperture and edge technologies to reduce detection and engagement by 50 percent.

The center and aft fuselage of the proposed upgrade was similar in size to the F-117A, but with structural strengthening. The Navy version weighed four and one-half tons more than the original version, with maximum take-off weight estimated at about 65,700 pounds. The F-117N was still under construction during 1996.

But even as the new F-117 version was being debated, a number of improvements were made to the F-117A fleet following its Desert Storm duties. The 1992 fiscal year defense authorization approved $83 million for those upgrades. The package included upgrading the mission planning system's user interface. The main portion of the upgrade included the addition of the Global Positioning System, which provided low probability-of-intercept, aircraft-to-aircraft communications, and an all-weather capability.

The early 1990s saw the F-117 Offensive Capability Improvement Program, which included improved computers and the installation of Digital Tactical Displays and automatic throttles for cruise control.

Another improvement made to the F-117 fleet came in the form of a new composite material installed on wing trailing edges. The space-age material, called AFR700B, increased the maximum operating temperature for composite materials. It was developed by Wright Laboratory at Wright Patterson AFB.

In the mid-1990s, the Air Force undertook a program to rapidly improve the accuracy of high-altitude bombing. The initiative called for the development of a Wind Corrected Munitions Dispenser (WCMD), which would allow the dispensing of cluster munitions while flying out of range of enemy air defenses. The F-117 was one of the aircraft which would receive the new capability. The Air Force indicated that it hoped the capability would be in place by 1999.

The Air Force's thinking of today shows a long career for the Nighthawks, with retirement in the 2018 time period. Looks like a long line of duty for this magnificent machine!

In 1993-1994, USAF generals were insistent about the need for additional F-117s. They pointed to the fact that even though the F-117s represented only a small percentage of the total force, they were used in virtually all strikes against the highest-priority targets in the Persian Gulf War. The highly-publicized success of the aircraft in those missions certainly didn't hurt the argument. Still, in the mid-1990s there was still no action on that proposal.

Also from the publisher

LOCKHEED F-94 Starfire
A Photo Chronicle

David R. McLaren & Marty Isham

The first U.S. night/all-weather fighter aircraft is chronicled, as is its use by Air Defense Command, Continental Air Command, and Alaska and North-East Air Command, and the Air National Guard.
Size: 8 1/2" x 11" over 220 b/w and color photographs
128 pages   soft cover
ISBN: 0-88740-451-0 $19.95

ROCKWELL B-1B
SAC's LAST BOMBER

Don Logan

This new book covers the complete history of the B-1 Lancer from its inception, through production, and operations with Strategic Air Command.
Size: 8 1/2" x 11" over 400 color & b/w photographs, line drawings, index
256 pages, hard cover
ISBN: 0-88740-666-1 $49.95

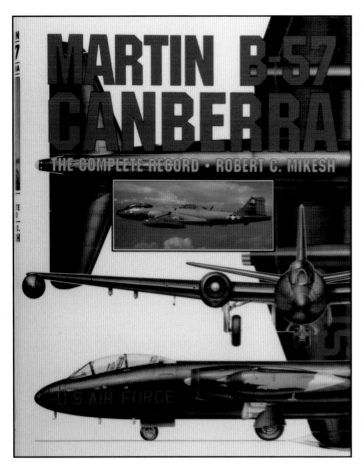

MARTIN B-57 Canberra
The Complete Record

Robert C. Mikesh

A brief history of its British inception sets the stage for the conversion to
American standards for production in the United States. The Canberra
was needed to fill the night intruder role in the USAF that was identified
during Korea and later Vietnam.
Size: 8 1/2" x 11" over 420 color & b/w photographs
208 pages, hard cover
ISBN: 0-88740-661-0 $45.00

TAIL CODE
The Complete History of USAF
Tactical Aircraft Tail Code Markings

Patrick Martin

Full color history covers PACAF, TAC, AFRES, ANG, AAC, USAFE codes
and markings.
Size: 8 1/2" x 11"   240 pages   hard cover, over 300 color photos
ISBN: 0-88740-513-4 $45.00